The BEER LOVER'S *Bible*
& HOME BAR HANDBOOK

Also by Nic van Oudtshoorn
and published by TAKE THAT BOOKS

The Hangover Handbook and Boozer's Bible

Please see page 96 for ordering details

The
BEER LOVER'S
Bible
& HOME BAR HANDBOOK

NIC VAN OUDTSHOORN

TAKE THAT BOOKS

THE BEERLOVER'S BIBLE

For my Daphne... and her elephants
With love

Take That Books is an imprint of
Take That Ltd.
P.O.Box 200
Harrogate
HG1 4XB

Copyright © 1993 Take That Books
& Maximedia Pty Ltd, Australia.

Cartoons: SHANE SUMMERTON

Published by arrangement with:
MaxiBooks, P.O.Box 268, Springwood, NSW 2777, Australia.

10 9 8 7 6 5 4 3 2 1

All rights reserved around the world. This publication is
copyright and may not be reproduced in whole or in part in any
manner (except excerpts thereof for bona fide purposes in
accordance with the Copyright Act) without the prior consent
in writing from the publisher.

This is a work of humour and of fiction. Under no circumstances should anybody act on material given in this book.
The publisher, author, and their respective employees or agents,
shall not accept responsibility for injury, loss or damage occasioned
by any person acting or refraining from action as a result of
material in this book whether or not such injury, loss or damage is
in any way due to any negligent act or omission, breach of duty or
default on the part of the publisher, author, or their respective
employees or agents.

ISBN 1-873668-30-9

Layout and typesetting by
Impact Design, P.O.Box 200, Harrogate, HG1 4XB.

Printed and bound in Great Britain.

AND HOME BAR HANDBOOK

THE BEERLOVER'S BIBLE

Contents

Here's to Beer! 6
Beer in Britain 7
Brew your own - it's fun 12
Tasting a beer 18
Beer and Sex 21
In a can, a bottle or on draught? 23
When in Rome... 28
The gentle art of pouring 31
Did you know...? 33
What a way to have a beer! 34
Beer heroes of history 39
From barbie to banquet 44
Weird beer facts & feats 50
Beer lover's bar quiz 53
Tegestology 55
Home bar entertaining 56
A note on potency 64
International beers 66
Glossary of beer terms 89
Answers to the Beer Lover's Quiz .. 94

AND HOME BAR HANDBOOK

Here's to Beer!

Beer, beer - glorious beer! It's *"a dish fit for a king,"* said Shakespeare - and today billions around the world agree with heady delight, while quaffing their way through thousands of different brands of this golden brew.

ORIGINS

But where did beer or ale originate? Popular opinion usually points to Britain as being the home of beer, but historians have always thought this to be most unlikely.

In 1992, scientists working in Iran uncovered a jar at Goden Tepe which was carbon dated as coming from late 4,000 BC. The grooves of the jar were found to contain a substance known as calcium oxalate. This is the main component of 'beerstone' which is a deposit left by drinks brewed from barley. Although these oxalates could have come from other products, such as rhubarb, it is considered most unlikely that the jar would have been used to store anything other than liquid - in other words, a fermented barley drink.

The brewers of this drink were Sumerians, one of the oldest literate civilisations. They em-

ployed a relatively complicated system of agriculture utilising irrigation to grow cereal crops including barley.

To convert the starch found in barley into a soluble form, the Sumerians probably made bread! A sourdough will have been added to the fresh barley and the resultant mixture made into loaves. These loaves, when broken up and added to water, would have fermented easily.

BEER IN BRITAIN

The fermented drink produced by the Sumerians would strictly have been called an 'ale'. Although the fermentation process is similar, to produce 'beer' requires the use of hops.

Cereals were being cultivated in Britain when the Romans conquered the country in 55BC. So it is likely that some of the barley being grown in this period was used to produce ale.

The modern word *'Ale'* is possibly derived from the Norse word *'Öl'*, which was used for their own Viking brew made from a large red berry found growing wild in many parts of Scandinavia.

In Saxon times the word *'beor'* was used to describe inferior mead (fermented honey and water), but this word seemed to disappear from the language for around 500 years.

Hops were not introduced into Britain until the 1500's. They were initially grown by Flemish settlers in Kent. So it is likely that even the production of true *'beer'* originated on the continent, probably in the Benelux region.

A CLOSER LOOK

So what is this amazing liquid we call beer - and what about such close relatives as ale and stout? Why are some beers light-coloured and others dark, some mind-blowingly potent and some extra mild, some old and others new? And how do master brewers create such an amazing range of tastes using four classic ingredients: barley, hops, yeast and water?

As described above, beer is made from the brewing and fermentation of cereals, usually malted barley, and flavoured with hops to give it a bitter taste. Fungus yeast converts the sugars in the malted barley to alcohol. But if the alcohol content gets too high it kills the yeast, making it impossible to brew very strong beer.

Traditional beer and ale are top fermented (that is, the yeast floats on the top), while lager (the most widely drunk beer in the world today) is bottom fermented. Lager - which means "storage" - was first brewed in a Bavarian monastery in the 14th century and because it needs a low fermentation temperature lagers were brewed next to lakes that froze over in winter, until the invention of refrigeration. Lagers are light coloured, have a medium hop flavour, dry taste, high carbonation and an alcohol content usually between 3% & 4% by volume.

Top fermented beers, which are particularly popular in Britain, include ale, stout and porter.

Stout was originally brewed - and called *"stoutt"* - as a thick and very potent drink which was served like a liqueur in small fluted glasses. Women loved this drink, because it was supposed to keep their shape in the way men then thought attractive. It helped them maintain

a kind of buxom stoutness which artists like Rubens and Rembrandt painted with such delight. The drink was gradually thinned down into the stout we know today, perhaps to keep up with female fashion for a thinner form. Stout gets its dark colour from roasted barley or malt which is included with the normal malt and other ingredients before mashing.

Think of stout and most people today think of Guinness, Ireland's most famous export which, it is claimed, gets its soft and special taste from certain springs in the County Kildare, before being allowed to mature for a year in oaken vats.

Ale and stout have a stronger, more hoppy flavour than lager and their alcohol content usually ranges between 4-6.5 % by volume.

In Germany, since 1615, only barley, hops, yeast and water have been used for brewing hundreds of different varieties of beer, following the promulgation of the Pure Beer Law by Count William IV of Bavaria.

Not so in countries such as Australia. A New South Wales Act of 1850 aimed to curb some of the worst concoctions which were being sold as beer. A brewer faced a then substantial fine of £200 and confiscation of his stock if he should add to his brew *"any vitriol, coculus indicus, nux vomica, tobacco, opium, aloes, copperas, faba amara or any extract or preparation thereof..."* And if you're wondering about *"nux vomica"*... it's another term for strychnine!

Other additives used in the past were also quite detrimental to the health of heavy drinkers, such as cobalt salts used in the 1960s (but now abandoned) to improve beer's foaming qualities.

Additives allowed for beer today are: propylene glycol alginate, sulphur dioxide, ascorbic acid or erythorbic acid, caramel, tannic acid, papain, bromelin and ficin.

Today there is a big trend towards pure beer, which relies on traditional ingredients and the brewmaster, rather than additives, to achieve great taste. The champions of this cause are The Campaign for Real Ale (CAMRA), started by a group of friends in Britain in 1971 out of enthusiasm for cask-conditioned ale. CAMRA has now turned into a respected consumer organisation and is regularly consulted by the media on all beer subjects.

Brew your own - it's fun

 BREWING your own beer has never been cheaper, easier or more fun. Take the right care and attention, and after a little bit of experience you'll be brewing one of the best drops you've ever tasted. That's guaranteed!

The first question many new home brewers face is: how much can I brew legally? In Britain, you can brew any amount of beer at any alcoholic strength as long as you don't sell a drop of it.

The main utensils you need to brew beer at home are:

✓ **A boiler** that holds at least 10 litres of water, preferably more. Most home brewers prefer boilers made from aluminium with two handles for easy lifting. Do not use bare copper or lead containers.

✓ **Fermentation vessels.**

A plastic garbage container is good for an open fermenter, for use with top fermenting yeast. You can also use this for bottom fermenting yeasts, but the container will need to be sealed with a sheet of plastic and secured with an elastic band. It is best, however, to use a special closed fermenter fitted with a fermentation lock.

No matter which yeast you use, it is best to ferment your beer in two stages. The first stage is performed in the open fermenter, for about two to five days, until the vigorous initial fermentation subsides. You then rack (syphon) the beer into the closed fermenter for the next stage; this leaves the sediment behind. Plastic pipes with an internal diameter of about 1cm are ideal for syphoning.

To avoid the need to strain the wort, it is a good idea to tie the hops in a muslin bag.

✓ **Thermometer and hydrometer.**

Keeping your brew within the correct temperature range is essential for proper fermentation. A hydrometer reading of below 1006 in an open fermenter will tell you when fermentation is complete, but it is easy enough to see when the brew starts to clear.

A good way to start this fascinating hobby is to buy one of the many commercial home brew kits which are readily available. Each comes with detailed instructions, so here is a summary of what is involved:

1 Carefully sterilise all the equipment you'll be using including bottles with sodium metabisulphite. Dissolve one heaped teaspoon in 500ml of warm water, then soak all the brewing utensils in this, including your bottles. Make sure you rinse all the utensils.

2 Open the can, which contains the malt and hops extract called the wort, and dissolve the mixture in hot water. Rainwater is best for this, although you should boil all water before using it for brewing. If the water is too soft, you can harden it with calcium sulphate (one teaspoon for every 22.5 litres).

3 Pour the mixture into the fermenting vessel, which usually has a 22.5 litre (5 gallon) capacity.

4 Determine how potent you want your beer to be, then dissolve 500 grams to one kilogram of sugar (the more sugar, the greater the alcohol content, but only up to a point) in hot water.

5 Pour the sugar solution into the fermenting vessel.

6 Top up the fermenting vessel with cold water.

7 Add the yeast which comes with the kit.

8 Fit the airlock.

9 Place in an area with a temperature of between 23ºC and 27ºC (the area near a hot water system is usually ideal).

10 After five days, pour the liquid into well-sterilised bottles (leave about 2.5cm at the top for air or the bottles will burst) and add a teaspoon of sugar to each bottle to provide the sparkle and head to your final brew.

11 Use a wooden capper to seal the bottles with crown seals.

12 Place the bottles in a warm spot for about five days, then store for around two months.

13 Enjoy your first of many great brews.

If you're the kind of purist who doesn't trust kits and prefers to make your own from scratch, here are some recipes which have produced great home brews for many. Again, make sure every item you plan to use is thoroughly sterilised; failure to do so could spoil your brew.

Basic Brew

60g hops
1000g malt extract
1000g sugar (equal parts of white and brown)
1 teaspoon salt
1 teaspoon citric acid
1 teaspoon top-fermenting yeast
20 litres water

Dissolve malt, sugar, salt and hops in 5-10 litres of water, bring to boil and simmer for 30 minutes. Place the remainder of the water and the citric acid in the fermenter (open or closed type). Add the boiling liquid to this.

Cool to below 27°C (ideal fermenting temperatures are 16°C to 21°C.). Add yeast. Skim twice a day until the frothing stops. Place one teaspoon of sugar in each bottle, then pour in the liquid. Cap the bottles. Store in a warm place (23°C-27°C) for a few days, then mature for four to eight weeks.

Light Lager

60g hops
1500g malt extract
500g sugar (equal parts of white and brown)
125g crystal malt
half a teaspoon salt
1 teaspoon citric acid

1 teaspoon lager (bottom-fermenting) yeast
20 litres water

Dissolve malt, sugar, salt and hops in 5-10 litres of water, bring to boil and simmer for 30 minutes. Place the remainder of the water and the citric acid in a closed-type fermenter. Add the boiling liquid to this.

Cool to below 27°C. Add bottom-fermenting lager yeast. Skim twice a day until the frothing stops. Wait 24-36 hours, then place water into the fermentation lock. When fermentation is complete, wait a few days for the beer to clear.

Place one teaspoon of sugar in each bottle, then pour in the liquid. Cap the bottles. Store in a warm place (23°C-27°C.) for a few days, then mature for at least four weeks.

THE BEERLOVER'S BIBLE

TASTING A BEER

WHETHER YOU'VE BREWED IT YOURSELF, or paid out hard earned cash over a bar, you will have your own way of appreciating beer. But what should you be looking for? We can all spot a good picture, but how many of us could recognise a Monet or Rubens? However, the sheer range of beers and refined flavours available means that what you should look for in one beer would be completely unacceptable in another. Bearing that in mind, a generalisation can be made.

First of all, the pint of beer must look good. The colour should be what you are expecting: A pilsner will be clear and golden, whilst a stout

AND HOME BAR HANDBOOK

will be opaque and almost black. The head should be rich and creamy, deep and uneven.

Secondly, the bubbles should be small - large bubbles often indicate a beer that has not finished fermentation. And there should be no 'bite' reflected in the overall taste from the carbonate.

An interwoven residue should be left on the glass as the beer retreats to the bottom. This is termed *'Brussels Lace'* by the brewers.

Unless you are drinking a deliberately sedimented beer, it should be clear. Note that many beers contain sediment in the bottle, such as many Belgian Trappist brews, but it should stay right there, in the bottle. Skill is required in opening the bottle and pouring the beer without disturbing the sediment. German Wheat beers, on the other hand, are meant to be served with a suspension of yeast.

The beer should have a distinctive aroma or 'bouquet'. This will be particular to the beer, but could be fruity, hoppy, herbal or malty.

As with most things these days, beer has become subjected to many rules and regulations. Did you know that the European Brewing Convention has units for Colour and Bitterness taste, plus an agreed range of 120 descriptions that can be used for the taste?

In the colour stakes, a Pilsner will have around 5-10 units of colour, while a Porter could have 80-100 units!

Whereas, when it comes to bitterness, a beer with 10-20 units of bitterness would be termed 'bland', a beer with 40 units or more would be overpoweringly well flavoured.

Even carbonation is quantified, one 'volume' of carbonation being equal to 2gm/litre. A range of one to three would cover most beers and lagers.

You will, of course, have your own tastes. Who cares if you can't identify the Monet or Rubens, if the picture looks good that's all that matters. It is also amazing how you can find the brighter points of your own brew while everybody else is heading for the kitchen sink!

STRONG BREWS

The most potent beer in the world is Roger & Out, with 16.9% alcohol by volume and an Original Gravity of 1125°. It has been brewed at the Frog & Parrott in Sheffield since 1985.

The strongest, as measured by original gravity is The Doomsday Ale brewed by the Cornish Brewery Company with an alcohol content of 15.9% by volume and an Original Gravity of 1143.5°.

When it comes to lagers, the strongest available is reputedly Samichlaus dark 1987 which was brewed by Brauerei Hurlimann in Switzerland. It contained 14.9% alcohol by volume and had an Original Gravity of 1123°.

Beer and Sex

WANT TO DRINK A LOT OF BEER AND STILL BE IN THE MOOD FOR LOVE? Then a French brewery may have some good news for you real soon. A heady announcement said the brewery had started tests on a beer, said to contain natural aphrodisiacs, that does not affect the drinker's ability for making love. The beer, it continued, was being tested under strict medical control by 400 drinkers. Explained Technical Director Marc Arbogast: *"It is not a product for Don Juan or marathon love makers, but is meant for men who have experienced sexual inhibitions."*

Amazingly, the beer is not very potent (as you would expect for it to release all those inhibitions), but is a mild barley brew with only about 2.5 per cent alcohol, about the same as a typical low-alcohol lager.

"Alcohol is known for its effect of sapping virility and this should reverse the effects," the director added.

So where can you buy this amazing brew? Nowhere yet and the fact that the news story was published on April Fool's Day should give you some idea of when it is likely to be available. Although the brewery, of course, denied strenuously that it was playing a practical joke on beer-loving lovers.

And while on the subject of sex, a few years ago *Pageant* magazine, under the headline **Distinguished Doctors Name the Eight Foods That Spark Sexual Desire**, reported:

"Peculiarly, of the commonly available foods, beer is the most likely to give women a boost in basic femininity... The hop is one of the few foods actually containing oestrogens..."

Beer belly blues ...

Why do fervent beer drinkers so often develop beer bellies? It's all the fault of beer's great relaxing qualities, caused by valerianic acid (a relation of Valium). It relaxes your muscles, particularly in the stomach and if you drink too much of the good stuff, your belly muscles remain permanently relaxed.

IN A CAN, A BOTTLE OR ON DRAUGHT?

THE METHOD OF STORING A BEER can be almost as important as the way it is brewed in the first place. With the exception of the sedimented beers, like many of the Belgians, beer is vulnerable to going-off from the moment it leaves the brewery. Unlike a wine, a beer should not be 'laid down' to mature.

A beer can 'go-off' in many ways, but the two most common are by reaction to light and oxidisation. Exposure to strong light, such as in a supermarket, can cause a bottled beer to obtain a cabbagey taste and smell. Oxidisation, by way of contact with the air, will cause a stale taste.

To overcome the above problems, always store your beers in a cool, but not cold, dark cellar - in the garage or under the stairs in most households. If it is in a bottle with a metal or plastic cap store upright so the brew doesn't contact the cap. If, however, the bottle is sealed with a cork, you should store it horizontally so the beer is in contact with the cork. This keeps the cork moist and prevents it contracting and allowing air in through the cracks.

Bad Can

Should you buy your beer in cans, bottles or on draught? As with all matters beer, this is not an easy question to answer. There is no firm evidence, but many brewers believe the prolonged contact of their beer with metal produces - wait for it - a metallic taste.

However, if you have just drunk a 'bad can', it is more than likely that a poor batch of beer has been produced and the brewers have sent it out in cans rather than through the trade. This practice, although denied, is common because cans are less likely to be returned than a pint in a pub or beer in a bottle - after all, its the fault of the metal, isn't it?!

Bottled beer is more likely to be pasteurised than draught beer, so the draught version will taste fresher. This, of course, is dependent on the publican rotating his stock correctly and keeping his lines clean. Also, in a low turnover pub, the beer will suffer from the lack of pasteurisation.

The final decision to be made, assuming you've opted for a draught beer, is should you have a half-pint or a full pint, and should you take it in a straight glass or a glass with a handle? If you are on a tasting session, it is probably better to go for the half-pints. In that manner, your palate will remain more sensitive to differences - not to mention your head! As for the shape of the glass, the main difference is likely to be your own preferences. However, it has been argued that a straight glass helps the carbonate evolve and move up the glass easier.

Horny drinkers made a tumbler

A tumbler today is associated with drinking water rather than beer, yet its name is directly related to the golden brew. In Anglo-Saxon days drinking horns were used by beer-loving warriors - and tradition demanded the ale or beer had to be drained with one gulp.

To stop anyone cheating, the horns had rounded bottoms so that when you put one down it would tumble - and spill any ale left inside for all to see. The first glass glasses followed this round-bottomed pattern and so became known as *"tumblers"* - and the name stuck even when they acquired flat bottoms.

"Give me a woman who truly loves beer, and I will conquer the world."
- KAISER WILHELM OF GERMANY

THE BEERLOVER'S BIBLE

Gulp, gulp, gulp ... splash...!

Today the closest we have to a drinking horn is the Ale-yard; a trumpet-shaped glass vessel, exactly a yard in length, with a closed narrow end which is expanded into a large ball.

It usually holds around two pints, and when filled with ale or beer the challenge is to empty the entire yard without taking it away from your mouth at all.

This is far from easy. For, so long as the tube contains beer, it flows out smoothly, but when air reaches the bulb it displaces the beer with a splash, startling the drinker so that he involuntarily withdraws his mouth. The result? Cold beer all over his face and clothes!

A favoured technique to overcome the 'bulb - splash' is to slowly rotate the yard, thus creating a small vortex in the bulb and allowing the ale to wash gently down the stem.

Puzzle out this holy fug

If you thought a yard was hard going, try sampling a Wager or Puzzle fug. In the 17th century these strange beer mugs, illustrated left, were great favourites at country inns. They usually had many spouts, from most of which it was difficult to drink - owing to holes in the neck.

Those in the know used to slurp up the liquor through a secret passage in the hollow handle or through one spout or nozzle - if the drinker had enough fingers to stop up the other spouts and holes during the operation! On many of these jugs were challenging inscriptions, like this one:

From Mother Earth I claim my birth,
I'm made a joke to man,
But now I'm here, fill'd with good beer
Come, taste me if you can.

Is drinking beer a mug's game?

Germans have a huge range of beer steins, the biggest of which holds four litres. The closest we can come to that is the ordinary beer mug. But have you ever wondered why we call it a *"mug"*? If you've ever seen a Toby jug, you'll guess the answer. Actually, the term started in 18th century England where patrons brought their own mugs to alehouses - which soon became known as mughouses - and left them there. Each mug was uniquely identified with its owner, so anyone's face (his or her unique feature) became known as their *"mug"*.

When in Rome...

Ever watched a Frenchman drink a beer? Or a Pole? They certainly all do it differently and well-travelled beer lovers say not much has changed since the *American Bottler* published this fascinating report on how the different nationalities drink their amber drop:

The Englishman

...always drinks standing; he waits until the froth gets off, and then, keeping his eyes on the bottom of the tumbler, never lets go until the last drop has gone down, saying, as he sets down the glass, *"Well, 'Enry, that's tol'ble."*

The Frenchman

...prefers to sit on the back of a chair, if such a place is handy by; he sips once or twice, and then waits; he sips again, and then says *"sacre"*, and then with a grande gulp, the whole quantity goes down.

The Yankee

...rushes in as if just off the express, invites every occupant of the room to drink, gives his elbow a twist that makes only one swallow of a glass, and wiping his mouth with his coat sleeve, calmly says, *"Frank, just charge that to my personal account"*.

THE BEERLOVER'S BIBLE

The Irishman
...had rather lean against the bar. He drinks slowly, so that the sensation will last as long as possible, and, when through, smilingly asks the barman if it wouldn't *"now ben a foine thing for you to treat me with a glass"*.

The Pole
...steps lightly up to the counter, deposits his money in advance, bows and looks so pleasant while drinking that you might imagine he wishes every sort of good luck to the man who first substituted beer for cold water.

The Spaniard
...walks in a stern, defiant air, looks all around as though counting noses, and then drinks alone. If the beer is good, he will say he

never drank worse; if bad, he will sooner fight than pay for it.

The German

...walks in as if it were a big effort; sits down on the nearest chair, and looks all over the room, then takes out a big pipe and fills and lights it.

In about half an hour he calls for some beer ...in from three to five minutes he thinks he will take a little lager ...in about ten minutes he wants to talk, and he believes he will take a little lager beer; talking reminds him that he wants some more beer ...in the course of an hour he will eat some pretzels and bologna, and there's nothing like beer to wash down the crumbs ...he thinks of going, and takes a little lager ...he gets up to go, and takes a little beer ...he asks for the beer, and makes the change in his favour by a big glass of lager beer.

Exclaiming as he goes out, *"Mein switzer pretzel dunder blitzen himmel zweigetenburgowhelfrankerfelternein"* - which means that he will be in by-and-by to get a glass of beer.

Did you know...?

In Western Australia you can order "A Pony" of beer, which is five fluid ounces (140ml).

If that is too much, you can also order "A Shetland" - presumably a small Pony - which is four fluid ounces (115ml)!

The gentle art of pouring

A good beer - and that surely includes your favourite drop - deserves to be served at the right temperature and in a way that best brings out its full flavour.

So, unless your thirst is desperate, don't drink straight from the bottle or can. Instead, use a glass or a beer mug, which allows the excess carbon dioxide to escape. The trick is to gently pour most of the beer down the side of the slightly tilted glass or mug, with the last part poured down the middle to give the beer a full head and enhance its bouquet.

When serving home brew, pour with great care to avoid any of the sediment getting into the glass. Here's how to do it:

- ✓ Line up the glasses and carefully remove the bottle cap.
- ✓ Tilt the first glass, then pour the beer slowly down the side, bringing the glass vertical as it fills up.
- ✓ Put down the full glass but keep the bottle tilted.
- ✓ Repeat with the other glasses until just before you reach the sediment, then stop.

Using the right glasses is an important part of running a home bar and the first essential rule is never to use your beer glasses or mugs for anything other than beer. No matter how well you wash the glasses or mugs, foreign substances such as milk will stick to the glass and, even in minute quantities, will contaminate your beer, adversely affecting the taste.

When you wash your beer glasses, don't use detergent or soap. Instead, wash them in a very hot solution of baking soda or salt, then rinse in clean hot water. Don't use a cloth for washing or drying, but allow the mugs and glasses to air dry.

We all know that beer shouldn't be too effervescent, and that it should be served cool but not cold. While in Australia they love nothing better than a freezing fizzy lager. So what's the right temperature?

Experts say **the ideal temperature** for serving lager is 5.5°C; for all-malt beers 8°C to 10°C; for ale and stout (including Guinness) 12.7°C.

But in the end your personal taste must determine the temperature at which you like your favourite brew. An ice-cold beer may sound good, but freezing it is one certain way to spoil a brew. When an all-malt beer is served below 7°C. it will develop *"chill haze"*; this makes the beer hazy, but will usually clear when the temperature rises.

Did you know...?

It's usual to dismiss an unimportant person as "small beer". But where does the term come from? It does not relate to a small quantity of beer, but to the weakest brew, which in Merrie Olde England was called "Small Beer" (or, deprecatingly, "Starve Gut").

Strong beer, which cost more and was known as Dragon's Milk, Merry-go-down or Humming Ale (from the way it made your head feel), was considered more important to serious drinkers.

What a way to have a beer!

NEED AN EXCUSE TO HAVE A BEER? Then why not blow your money - and get your mates to stage a *"Bede-ale"* to restore your fortunes! Bede-ale was a medieval male custom very much like the Australian concept of mateship.

If an honest man suffered a financial setback, through no fault of his own, the law allowed his friends to drink him back to prosperity!

The publican, by law, had to hand over a certain percentage of all the money the drinkers spent during this Bede-ale session to the victim. The bigger the financial loss, of course, the longer and drunker the party. And, because it was permitted by law, no wife dared complain!

Other old customs involving beer drinking were Bid-Ales, Bride-Ales, Give-Ales, Cuckoo-Ales, Help-Ales, Tithe-Ales, Leet-Ales, Lamb-Ales, Midsummer-Ales, Scot-Ales, and Wedden-Ales.

Here comes the bride - bearing beer

Bride-Ale was the English custom of the bride selling ale on the wedding day, for which she received any sum or present which her friends chose to give her.

And what parties these weddings were! One account from 1545 notes matter-of-factly: *"When they came home from the church, then beginneth excesse of eatying and drynking, and as much is waisted in one daye as were sufficient for the two newe-married folkes half a yeare to lyve upon."*

Egg on your mug

Egg Ale was a somewhat remarkable - and, on the face of it, a slightly revolting - concoction, although said to be highly nutritious. The old recipe stipulated:

To twelve gallons of ale was added the gravy of eight pounds of beef. Twelve eggs, the gravy beef, a pound of raisins, oranges and spice, were then placed in a linen bag and left in the barrel until the ale had ceased fermenting. Even then an addition was made in the shape of two quarts of Malaga sack. After three weeks in cask the ale was bottled, a little sugar being added. A monstrously potent liquor truly!

A cock and beer story!

Ever tasted a Beer Cup? It certainly is a novel way to drink your beer - although few beer lovers today are likely to mix their favourite drink that way. Popular at the beginning of the 18th Century, we read of Beer Cups with names like Humpty-dumpty, Clamber-clown, Hugmatee, Stick-back, Cock Ale and Knock-me-down. Cock Ale, hailed as *"a very strengthening and restorative compound"*, was made this way:

Take a cock of half a year old, kill him and truss him well, and put into a cash twelve gallons of ale to which add four pounds of raisins of the sun, well picked, stoned, washed and dryed; sliced Dates, half a pound; nutmegs and mace two ounces: Infuse the dates and spices in a quart of canary twenty-four hours, then boil the cock in a manner to a jelly, till a gallon of water is reduced to two quarts; then press the body of him extremely well, and put the liquor into the cask where the ale is, with the spices and fruit, adding a few blades of mace; then put to it a pint of new ale yeast, and let it work well for a day, and, in two days, you may broach it for use or, in hot weather, the second day; and if it proves too strong, you may add more plain ale to palliate this restorative drink, which contributes much to the invigorating of nature.

These strange concoctions were served into small glasses from containers called posset pots, delicate glass bowls with one or two handles.

THE BEERLOVER'S BIBLE

Flip me a drop, please!

Flip, a very popular drink for our ancestors, is made this way, according to an old recipe:

Place in a saucepan one quart of strong ale together with lumps of sugar which have been well rubbed over the rind of a lemon, and a small piece of cinnamon. Take the mixture off the fire when boiling and add one glass of cold ale. Have ready in a jug the yolks of six or eight eggs well beaten up with powdered sugar and grated nutmeg.

Pour the hot ale from the saucepan on to the eggs, stirring them while so doing. Have another jug at hand and pour the mixture as swiftly as possible from one vessel to the other until a white froth appears, when the flip is ready. One or two wine glasses of gin or rum are often added.

AND HOME BAR HANDBOOK

Top Five

The top five brewers in the world (by volume) are:-

1.	Anheuser	USA	9000 million litres
2.	Miller	USA	4720 million litres
3.	Heineken	Netherlands	4300 million litres
4.	Kirin	Japan	3100 million litres
5.	Bond	Australia	2900 million litres

Some of the better known brewers in Europe don't figure in this table because of the competition they face for their markets. Each German brewer, for instance, must compete with more than 1,000 other brewers.

Headstones

To the memory of Thomas Fletcher, a Grenadier in the North Battalion of the Hampshire Militia, who died of a fever, contracted by drinking small beer when hot, the 12th May 1764.

Here rests in peace a Hampshire Grenadier,
Who caught his death by drinking cold small beer;
Soldier, be warned by his untimely fall,
And when you're hot, drink strong, or none at all.

Poor John Stott lies buried here
Though once he was both hale and stout,
Death laid him on his bitter bier,
In another world he hops about.

THE BEERLOVER'S BIBLE

Beer heroes of history

WHO WAS THE GREATEST BEER DRINKER IN HISTORY? When it comes to free beers, there's no doubt the honour goes to a man named Jedediah Buxton, who throughout his life meticulously tallied up every beer anyone had ever bought him since he started drinking - at the age of 12!

Sixty years or so later the total came to an amazing 5116 pints, equal to about 10,000 cans. Jedediah claimed he could down a pint with only one breath - and won his free beers from those curious to see how many pints he could drink without losing his breath.

AND HOME BAR HANDBOOK

Thirsty Willie's grave problem

Beer certainly is healthy for you, but it can lead to a slight weight gain, as William Lewis discovered before his death in 1793. His obituary tells how Thirsty Willie made it a rule, every morning of his life, to read a number of chapters in the Bible and in the evening to drink eight gallons of ale.

"It is calculated," says one contemporary report, *"that in his lifetime he must have drunk a sufficient quantity to float a seventy-four gun ship. His size was astonishing, and he averaged 40 stone. Although he died in his parlour, it was found necessary to construct a machine in the form of a crane, to lift his body in a carriage, and afterwards to have the machine to let him down into the grave."*

Whether Willie left a bequest to buy the mourners a pint or two is not recorded.

Bountiful Bess's right royal treat

During the reign of Queen Elizabeth I, beer was divided into single beer, or small beer, double beer, double-double beer, and dagger ale, which was particularly sharp and strong.

Good Queen Bess, who served huge quantities of beer and ale at all Royal functions, drank her own special Royal Brew which was said to be so strong that no one else in the household could handle it.

This little piggy went to the pub!

Have you ever pigged out on beer? Then you'll have some sympathy with the unfortunate porcines belonging to home-brewing parson Rev. John Woodforde in 1765, who wrote with some astonishment in his diary:

"Brewed a vessell of strong Beer today. My two large Piggs, by drinking some Beer grounds taken out of one of my Barrels today, got so amazingly drunk by it, that they were not able to stand and appeared like dead things almost, and so remained all night from dinner-time today. I never saw Piggs so drunk in my life, I slit their ears for them without feeling... "

The next day the saga continued:

"My two Piggs are still unable to walk yet, but they are better than they were yesterday. They tumble about the yard and can be no means stand at all steady yet. Only this afternoon did they become tolerably sober..."

How the rector fared after drinking the actual brew that produced such potent grains is not recorded. Although his handwriting for a week was decidedly shaky...

Golden rule for golden ale

In ancient Mesopotamia Queen Shu-Bad thought so highly of beer that she would drink it only one way - by sipping it through a straw made of solid gold.

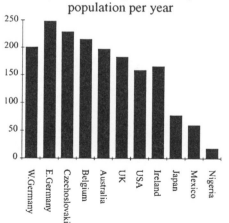

BEER CONSUMPTION
The average number of pints drunk per head of population per year

ALCOHOL CONSUMPTION

The total number of pints of 100% alcohol consumed per head per year

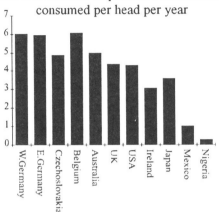

BEER COSTS

The average cost in pounds of a beer to an expatriate in each country (last available data 1988-90).
Foreigners could not officially buy beer in the former Eastern Bloc.

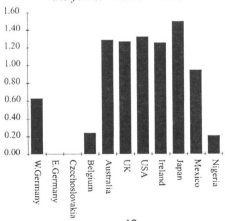

From barbie to banquet

BEER IS THE PERFECT DRINK for all occasions. For many, gulping down an ice-cold can of lager, or two, or three, on a boiling day or around the barbecue is the ultimate bliss. For others, a long lazy pint of 'best' following an afternoon in the garden is pure heaven. Yet when the same people go out to dinner, chances are they'll become conventional and order a wine with their meal.

Beer is a great drink at the dinner table - and with almost every kind of food, as our ancestors knew only too well.

In many parts of Europe, particular the cold northern regions, people for centuries began and ended their days with beer. As Michael Weiner points out in *The Taster's Guide to Beer*, the day began with *"a good draught to wet your whistle; at the noonday meal a beer soup; and at supper, of course, there must be egg-flip made with beer. Raisin beer and sugar beer, fish and sausages boiled in beer, beer in all conceivable forms, to say nothing of abundant draughts of plain beer when paying visits, talking business, attending baptisms and funerals..."*

England has always had a great tradition of serving beer with food. The following charges appear in the household expenses of King Henry VIII:

The queen's maids of honour to have a chet loaf, a manchet, a gallon of ale, and a chine of beef for their breakfast. The brewer is informed not to put any hops or brimstone in the ale.

Today, lovers of barbecues and Asian foods know the golden brew enhances the taste of meat and spicy dishes. But beer can compliment most other dishes as well. Just pick the correct brew and you can serve - and enjoy - beer with every course (except dessert, unless you are a real beer lover, that is!).

For pre-dinner drinks, offer your guests light, bitter, cold beer which will excite the gastric juices and work up an appetite.

Guinness goes down great with oysters served with brown bread, butter and lemon and with shellfish of every description.

For main courses, serve a strong, full-bodied beer (not too cold) with meat dishes and casseroles. Curries also call for a full-bodied strong brew, but much colder. With spicy Oriental food, a sweetish, light to medium beer is the ideal companion.

Of course, if you're a true beer lover, you'll also want to cook with beer. The Vikings of old loved their beer so much they included a soup made of their favourite brew with every meal and they ate six times a day!

Last century beer mixed with brown sugar was a favourite sauce for pancakes; red herrings were steeped in small beer before being broiled; and catsup (the forerunner of today's ketchup) for sea stores was made mainly of beer and vinegar.

Here's a few beer recipes to get you started:

Melon cocktail

Cut a large honeydew melon in half. Remove pips and scoop out balls. Place in a shallow dish and pour in beer until the melon balls are just covered. Stand for about 15 minutes, then put melon balls in cocktail glasses and cover them with chilled beer. Serves 6.

Beer Steak

500g rump steak
350ml beer
2 large onions
2 tablespoons butter
Salt and black pepper

Melt butter in shallow saucepan, add peeled and sliced onions and fry slowly until brown. Season steak, then place in saucepan on top of the onions. Cover and simmer on low heat for 90 minutes. Pour in the beer and continue simmering for two-and-a-half hours. Remove steak, thicken gravy with flour. Serve with mashed potatoes and vegetables.

Beer soup

600ml beer
600ml milk
2 egg yolks, beaten
1 teaspoon butter
half teaspoon salt
1 dessertspoon honey

Mix milk and beer, simmer for 15 minutes; add salt and honey; remove from heat and stir in butter and beaten egg yolks.

Seafood-'n-beer casserole

250g prawns, cooked and shelled
250g tinned crab meat
4 cups beer
24 oysters
2 onions

4 shallots
1 stick of sliced celery
1 teaspoon parsley
50g butter
1 tablespoon flour
salt and pepper to taste

In shallow saucepan, bring to boil the beer, onions, parsley, celery and shallots. Simmer for 15 minutes. Season with salt and pepper. Add prawns, oysters and crab meat. Mix flour and butter into a paste, then add to the saucepan and stir until boiling. Serve with rice.

Beer bread

1 cup beer
250g plain flour
1 cup wholemeal flour
2 tablespoons caster sugar
15g yeast

Take a loaf tin 20x10x8cm and grease. Cream the yeast and sugar in a warmed basin until liquid. Bring beer to boil, then allow to cool until tepid. Stir the beer into the yeast, then add butter and continue stirring with wooden spoon to a smooth dough. Brush with melted butter, then cover and leave in warm place until the dough doubles in size. Punch down. Cover, wait until it doubles in size again. Punch down again, then shape into the tin and cover the top with melted butter. Leave in warm place until double in size, then bake in moderate over (190°C., 375°F. for about one hour or until ready.

Ale and apple pie

600ml hot spiced ale
4 large cooking apples
2-3 tablespoons sugar
Grated peel of half lemon
Short pastry

Wash and core apples, then place them next to one another in a large pie dish. Mix butter, sugar and lemon peel into a firm paste. Pack into the cored hollows and smear surplus paste over the apple tops. Cover the dish with short pastry. Bake in hot oven (250°C., 450°F.) until pasty has risen. Lower to moderate (125°C.,350°F.) and bake until pastry is brown. Carefully remove pastry without breaking. Pour the hot spiced ale over the apples, cut the pastry into four and cover each apple with pastry. Serve with fresh cream.

Once, during Prohibition, I was forced to live for days on nothing but food and water.

- W.C. FIELDS

Weird beer facts & feats

Australian Graham Howard's Laidly Gold wheat beer is a real beauty bottler - literally so! It took 418.25 litres of the golden brew to fill the world's largest beer bottle at the Laidley Tourist Festival - and win Graham a spot in the *Guinness Book of Records*. The huge bottle, made specially for the occasion, stood 2.11 metres tall and had a circumference of 1.64 metres.

Graham's other pure wheat beers have such lip-smacking names as Brewhouse Old Bounty Ale and Settlers' Extra Stout.

Brewery magpies

There are many people around the world who believe (and rightly so!) that everything about beer is precious - so they collect a whole range of odds and ends relating to their favourite brew, from cans to labels and even beer mats.

The world's biggest collection of beer cans belongs to American John F. Ahrens of Mount Laurel, New Jersey, who has more than 15,000 cans from around the world. Australians, too, are fanatical beer can and bottle collectors, with the

Downer Club in Canberra recently paying AUS$25,000 for 2502 unopened bottles and cans from 103 countries at a charity auction.

When it comes to beer labels, there's no one to touch Norwegian Jan Solberg, whose collection totals more than 322,000! Austrian Leo Pisker, on the other hand, owns more than 130,000 beer mats from 153 countries.

Service with a five-headed smile

How's this for service? Barmaid Rosie Schedelbauer, carrying five full beersteins in every hand, dashed 15 metres to a world record in a mere four seconds in Germany in 1981.

And in England strongman Tommy Gaskin won himself a world record for raising a keg of beer weighing 62.5kg above his head 656 times in only 6 hours.

Here's a job to thirst after

During the Middle Ages, being an official Ale Taster was a job many beer lovers thirsted after. And no wonder: you could drink officially all day, then get paid in beer!

Noted one writer in 1617: *"John Shule and a patent from Arthur Lake, Bishop of Bath and Wells, and Vice-Chancellor of Oxford, for the office of ale-taster [to the University] and the making and assizing of barrels of beer. The office of ale tasting requires that he go to every ale-brewer that day they brew, according to their courses, and taste their ale; for which, his ancient fee is one gallon of strong ale and two gallons of small wort, worth a penny."*

Holy XXXX!

A letter of Pope Gregory to Archbishop Nidrosietisi, of Iceland, shows that in the 13th Century ale was so popular that some communities even used it to baptise their children! Wrote the wowser Pope: *"... since the heart ought to be born again of water and the Holy Spirit, those ought not to be considered as duly baptised who have been baptised in ale."*

'Ale and hearty

Ancient Egyptian doctors believed fervently in the value of beer to treat every kind of disease (including, of course, the occasional hangover). Archaeologists have found over 100 recorded medicines containing beer as the basic fluid.

Beer lover's bar quiz

BEER LOVERS should be authorities on their favourite drink - and what better way to impress your mates with your great knowledge than a quiz? Particularly if, thanks to *The Beer Lover's Bible and Home Bar Handbook*, you know all the answers (you can check with the correct answers on page 94).

1. Where is Kwak beer brewed?
2. Which Australian brew filled the world's largest beer bottle?
3. How could you once drink yourself to wealth with beer?
4. Who was the biggest beer freeloader in history?

5. Why did a bride traditionally sell beer on her wedding day in Merrie Olde England?
6. In which icy country did people once baptise their children with ale?
7. Who said: "Give me a woman who truly loves beer, and I will conquer the world"?
8. What is the ideal temperature for serving Lager?
9. What is 'nux vomica', once used in beer?
10. In which country did a queen sip her beer through a straw made of solid gold?
11. In which Australian State can you order a 'Shetland' of beer?
12. What is the alcohol content by volume of 'Roger & Out'?
13. Which beer-based drink would you serve in a posset pot?
14. Who are reputed to be the first people to make ale?
15. Which brewery is ranked fourth in the world on volume of beer produced?

THE BEERLOVER'S BIBLE

Tegestology

THE STUDY OR COLLECTION OF BEERMATS is known as Tegestology. The term is derived from the Latin word for 'rug' or 'mat' which is 'Teges'.

Beermats originated on the continent and were made from pottery or porcelain. By 1892 the first wood-pulp beermats were being produced in Germany, but it wasn't until 1920 that the first such mat was made in Britain. That distinction fell to Watney's of London who produced two different mats advertising their Pale Ale and Reids Stout.

These early mats were a lot thicker than today's variety. Most of those produced before 1935 were up to a quarter of an inch or six millimetres thick. Nowadays they are more likely to be only an eighth of an inch or three millimetres.

Over the years many brains, both great and small, sober and drunk, have sought further uses for the humble beermat. The aerodynamics have been utilised to turn it into a spinning weapon.

Anybody caught short needing to write down an important phone number or make a quick calculation can also turn to the beermat. Tests of dexterity include building beermat versions of card-houses, and flipping piles of beermats into the air from the edge of a table and catching them. And if the table proves to be uneven, one may be inserted under one of the legs to correct the situation.

AND HOME BAR HANDBOOK

Home bar entertaining

When it comes to entertaining at home, there's nothing to beat your own bar. Of course, being a beer lover, you'll ensure it's stocked with plenty of beer. But there's more to running a home bar than just serving - and drinking - beer. You'll need the following equipment for your bar:

Double-ended measuring cup
Lime-squeezer
Mixing spoon
Professional bar shaker with a wire strainer for cocktails
570ml glass beaker with pouring lip
Cutting board to prepare fruit for drinks
Sharp fruit knife
Ice bucket and ice crusher
Electric blender
If your budget permits, a small bar fridge.

In addition to a range of mixers, you'll need at least the following spirits:

Scotch whisky	Bourbon
Brandy	Coffee liqueur
Cointreau	Creme de Cacao

Galliano
Grenadine
Tequila
Vodka

Gin
Rum (white and dark)
Vermouth

The art of mixing cocktails

Generally, *'cocktails'* is accepted today as a generic term for all mixed drinks. Special glasses are not really necessary - almost any container, from a coconut shell to a pineapple, can be used to hold a cocktail attractively. As a guideline, however, choose stemmed glasses for cocktails which are not served on ice, as they will stay cooler longer, and tumblers or highball glasses for drinks which require ice. Short cocktails look their best in traditional triangular cocktail glasses, while goblet styles are generally used for drinks incorporating egg yolks.

All cocktails are served cold. It makes a great difference if the glasses have been chilled. Ideally the glasses should stand in the refrigerator for an hour or two before needed, but a scoop of ice placed in the glass and left there while the drink is being prepared will chill it very effectively.

Cocktails have a language all their own: when someone asks for one *"straight up"*, it means served without ice. Other terms you're likely to encounter are:

On the rocks - with ice

Strain - pour mix through strainer to remove ice chips and fruit

Twist - a small strip of lemon peel, sharply twisted to bruise the rind; this allows oil to escape into the drink when the peel is floated.

All cocktails must be measured carefully and as long as the measure remains constant throughout the recipe, the drink will have the correct flavour and consistency. Cocktails are made four ways:

Shaking

This method is usual for sweet-and-sour, sweet and cream-type drinks. You can use either cracked or cubed ice. Pour the ingredients into a cocktail shaker, add a handful of ice, shake briskly and serve as soon as the outside of the shaker begins to sweat.

Floating

This is done when a recipe calls for a cream or high-proof spirit to be floated on top of the mixed ingredients. Take a bar spoon (or a curved dessert spoon), hold it upside-down so the bottom touches the side of the glass, just above the other ingredients, then carefully pour the spirit or cream over it.

Stirring

This is for martini-type drinks where you want to make sure the base spirit is not bruised. Pour the ingredients into a 570ml glass beaker with a pouring lip, then stir with a clean bar spoon. Use ice blocks, not chips, and serve immediately before the ice dilutes the mixture.

Blending

If your recipe calls for fresh fruit or eggs, they will need to be blended to give them a frothy consistency. Pour the ingredients together with ice into an electric blender, then blend briefly. Never put a carbonated ingredient into your shaker, mixing glass or liquidiser. By the same token, glasses should not be filled to the brim - and remember to leave room for your garnish.

Cocktails should be served fresh as they will separate if left too long. Always hold the glass by the stem or the base to avoid fingerprints and unnecessary warming of the drink.

Dry Martini

Four parts gin   One part dry vermouth

Place four to six ice cubes into a mixing glass, add gin and vermouth. Stir carefully, and before ice starts to melt, strain into chilled cocktail glass. Garnish with lemon twist or green olive.

Singapore Sling

Created at the famous Raffles Hotel in Singapore in 1915, it calls for

Two parts gin   One part cherry brandy
One part orange juice   Soda Water
Dash bitters

Shake ingredients well with ice cubes. Pour into highball glass and top up with soda. Decorate with pineapple wedge and maraschino cherry.

White Lady

Two parts gin   Two parts cream
One part Creme de Cacao

Blend with crushed ice and strain into a small (90ml) martini glass.

Pimm's Royale

One part Pimm's No.1   Slice of orange
Two parts demi-sec champagne
or semi-sweet sparkling wine

Mix Pimm's and champagne, add ice and serve with a slice of orange.

Chi Chi

Three parts vodka   Two parts coconut cream
Eight parts pineapple juice
Two scoops crushed ice

Blend all ingredients together with the ice. Garnish with a slice of fresh pineapple and a cherry.

Nevada

Two parts under-proof rum   One part lime juice
Two prts grapefruit juice   One part sugar syrup

Shake together all ingredients.

Smiling Ivy

One prt under-proof rum   One prt peach liqueur
One part pineapple juice   Egg white
Dash lemon

Shake together all ingredients.

Rum Cocktail

45ml light rum   1 tsp of grenadine
2 tsps fresh lime/lemon juice   half tsp sugar

Blend or shake together very well. Serve straight up in a cocktail glass or on the rocks.

Old Fashioned

In an old fashioned glass dissolve 1 tsp of sugar in two dashes of Angostura bitters and a splash of club soda. Add two ice cubes and fill with dark rum. Decorate with fruit.

Screwdriver
Four parts orange juice   One part vodka
Pour vodka and orange juice over ice and serve.

Margarita
1 measure tequila   Dash Triple Sec
Juice of half a lime
Pour over crushed ice and stir. Rub the rind of the lemon on the rim of a stem glass, spin the rim in salt. Pour the drink into the glass and sip through the salt.

Brandy Flip
2 measures brandy   1 dash bitters
Half teaspoon curacao   Half teaspoon sugar
Lemon peel   1 sprig mint
Shake well, strain and serve.

Grasshopper
One-third measure creme de cacao
One-third green creme de menthe
One-third light sweet cream
Shake until very cold. Serve in tall glass.

Between the sheets
A quarter of a lemon   Half an ounce of rum
Half an ounce of brandy
Half an ounce of Triple Sec
Shake well with plenty of ice.

The tale behind the cocktail...

Some experts say the first recipe for a cocktail was a concoction of lemon juice and powdered adders, which was praised highly by the Emperor Commodus in the second century AD as an aperitif!

So where does the word cocktail come from? There are many stories, some more plausible than others. One traces it to an Aztec overlord in Mexico whose beautiful daughter was called X-octl. Some American officers went to visit her father and, after a pleasant meeting, were served some exotic mixed drinks. The officers said they would never forget X-octyl, so they decided to name the drinks after her. The closest they could come to pronouncing her name was *"cocktail"* - and a legend was born.

Another story says that during the American War of Independence, an innkeeper named Betsy Flanagan, whose premises were frequented by Lafayette's as well as Washington's officers, once prepared a meal of chickens she stole from a pro-British neighbour. To celebrate this small victory she decorated glasses used at the feast with feathers plucked from the chickens. Her French clients heartily toasted her with cries of *"Vive le cocktail!"*

The first true book of cocktails was by Jerry Thomas, who published in 1862 *The Bon Vivant's Guide or How to Mix Drinks.*

A note on potency

THE NUMBER OF METHODS of measuring the 'strength' of a beer - both ancient and modern - are almost as plentiful as the types of beers they are used to measure.

In the International Beer listings starting on page 66 of *The Beerlover's Bible and Homebar Handbook*, we have used the term 'Potency' in preference to 'Strength' since the latter is more often confused with the volume of alcohol contained in a beer. The measurement methods drop into two main categories; by alcoholic content, and by density.

In countries such as the USA and Canada, beers are expressed in alcohol per cent by weight or ABW. This produces a low number because alcohol is 'lighter' or less dense than water. More usual is the measurement of alcohol per cent by volume or ABV. This produces a slightly higher number for the same beer than the ABW. For example, an American beer may contain 32g of alcohol in 1000g of beer. This would occupy, more or less, 40cl per litre. The ABW would be 3.2% and the ABV 4.0%.

Traditional brewing nations such as Britain, Germany and Belgium often prefer to measure the potency of their beer by density, reporting the Original Gravity or Degrees Plato. This is a product of history when brewers could predict - for taxation purposes - the amounts of each raw material they would use for the brewing process. How much of this material would turn into alcohol was harder to predict.

Conversion between the various systems is often difficult because there can be a significant difference between the OG/Degrees Plato and the ABV depending on the degree of fermentation. However, the following very-rough rules of thumb may be used.

For converting between Original Gravity and Degrees Plato, take the last two figures of the OG and divide by four. For example, and beer with an OG of 1040 would equate to 10.0 degrees Plato.

You can often convert the OG directly into ABV, but this is a less accurate conversion. For example a 1040 OG would be approximately 4.0% ABV. However the same beer could quite easily be 3.8 - 4.2% ABV.

As a result, no attempt has been made to convert the potencies given in the International Beer list.

International beers
all you need to know

WHEN SERIOUS BEER LOVERS get together, it's not long before someone asks: *"And what do you think of..."* Instantly, your mind goes into overdrive, racing back through countless glasses, bottles and cans to recall that particular brew. Only then can you pontificate on the colour, head, texture, aroma and flavour, and make your judgement known - "a great drop, that, with a good rocky head, a slightly fruity aroma and a full-bodied texture, but perhaps a little sweet..."

Now, thanks to ***The Beerlover's Bible and Home Bar Handbook,*** you can carry with you a list of the world's most important beers and a brief summary of the beer, together with your own comments.

If you think we've missed out on your own favourite brew, and you think it is important enough that all other beer drinkers should know of its qualities, please write to us at the address in the front of this book. Hope you have as much fun sampling as we did. **CHEERS!!!**

AUSTRALIA

Swan Gold

Brewery: Swan
Colour: Light
Flavour: Fresh
Potency: 8 degrees

Date/place tasted: ....
Rating 1-10 (10=best): ....
Personal remarks: ....

Redback

Brewery: Matilda Bay
Colour: Pale gold
Flavour: Creamy
Potency: 1045 OG

Date/place tasted: ....
Rating 1-10 (10=best): ....
Personal remarks: ....

Coopers Sparkling Ale

Brewery: Coopers
Colour: Dark
Flavour: Earthy, dry
Potency: 1054 OG

Date/place tasted: ....
Rating 1-10 (10=best): ....
Personal remarks: ....

Cascade Sparkling Pale Ale

Brewery: Cascade
Colour: Golden
Flavour: Fresh
Potency: 11.7 degrees

Date/place tasted: ....
Rating 1-10 (10=best): ....
Personal remarks: ....

AUSTRIA

Hopfenperle

Brewery: Schwechat
Colour: Light
Flavour: Smooth, dry
Potency: 12.4 degrees

Date/place tasted: ....
Rating 1-10 (10=best): ....
Personal remarks: ....

Zipfer Urtyp

Brewery: Schwechat
Colour: Very pale
Flavour: Hoppy, aromatic
Potency: 12.5 degrees

Date/place tasted: ....
Rating 1-10 (10=best): ....
Personal remarks: ....

Gosser Stiftsbrau

Brewery: Styrian
Colour: Dark
Flavour: Sweet
Potency: 12.2 degrees

Date/place tasted: ....
Rating 1-10 (10=best): ....
Personal remarks: ....

Columbus

Brewery: Stiegel
Colour: Well hopped
Flavour: Malty, sweet
Potency: 13 degrees

Date/place tasted: ....
Rating 1-10 (10=best): ....
Personal remarks: ....

Ottakringer 150 Jahre

Brewery: Ottakringer
Colour: Reddish bronze
Flavour: Lightly sweet
Potency: 13 degrees

Date/place tasted: ....
Rating 1-10 (10=best): ....
Personal remarks: ....

Doppelhopfen Hell

Brewery: Baron Bachofen
Colour: Bronze
Flavour: Dry
Potency: 11 degrees

Date/place tasted: ....
Rating 1-10 (10=best): ....
Personal remarks: ....

ASIA

Singha

Brewery: Boon Rawd (Thailand)
Colour: Pale
Flavour: Unusual
Potency: 13.8 degrees

Date/place tasted: ....
Rating 1-10 (10=best): ....
Personal remarks: ....

Tiger

Brewery: Malayan Breweries
Colour: Golden
Flavour: Clean
Potency: 12 degrees

Date/place tasted: ....
Rating 1-10 (10=best): ....
Personal remarks: ....

BELGIUM

Gold Riband

Brewery: Liefmans
Colour: Dark
Flavour: Elegant
Potency: 13 degrees

Date/place tasted: ....
Rating 1-10 (10=best): ....
Personal remarks: ....

Pauwel Kwak

Brewery: Pauwel
Colour: Dark brown
Flavour: Licorice
Potency: 18.5 degrees

Date/place tasted: ....
Rating 1-10 (10=best): ....
Personal remarks: ....

De Koninck

Brewery: De Koninck
Colour: Golden
Flavour: Yeasty, fruity
Potency: 12 degrees

Date/place tasted: ....
Rating 1-10 (10=best): ....
Personal remarks: ....

Duvel

Brewery: Het Anker
Colour: Pale golden
Flavour: Clean, soft, fruity
Potency: 17.5 degrees

Date/place tasted: ....
Rating 1-10 (10=best): ....
Personal remarks: ....

Orval

Brewery: Orval
Colour: Orange
Flavour: Hoppy
Potency: 8.4% ABV

Date/place tasted: ....
Rating 1-10 (10=best): ....
Personal remarks: ....

Westmalle Dubbel

Brewery: Westmalle
Colour: Dark amber
Flavour: Rich maltiness
Potency: 16 degrees

Date/place tasted: ....
Rating 1-10 (10=best): ....
Personal remarks: ....

Westmalle Triple

Brewery: Westmalle
Colour: Amber
Flavour: Citric fruitiness
Potency: 20 degrees

Date/place tasted: ....
Rating 1-10 (10=best): ....
Personal remarks: ....

The Abbot

Brewery: Westvleteren
Colour: Dark
Flavour: Spicy, creamy
Potency: 21 degrees

Date/place tasted: ....
Rating 1-10 (10=best): ....
Personal remarks: ....

Chimay Red

Brewery: Chimay
Colour: Blackcurrant
Flavour: Reddish brown
Potency: 15.8 degrees

Date/place tasted: ....
Rating 1-10 (10=best): ....
Personal remarks: ....

Stella Artois

Brewery: Artois
Colour: Pale golden
Flavour: New mown hay
Potency: 5.2% ABV

Date/place tasted: ....
Rating 1-10 (10=best): ....
Personal remarks: ....

BRITAIN

Greenmantle Ale

Brewery: Broughton Brewery Ltd
Colour: Copper
Flavour: Rich maltiness
Potency: 4% ABV

Date/place tasted: ....
Rating 1-10 (10=best): ....
Personal remarks: ....

Theakstons Best Bitter

Brewery: Newcastle Breweries
Colour: Light
Flavour: Dry finish
Potency: 3.8% ABV

Date/place tasted: ....
Rating 1-10 (10=best): ....
Personal remarks: ....

Black Diamond

Brewery: Butterknowle
Colour: Ruby red
Flavour: Nutty, strong
Potency: 4.8% ABV

Date/place tasted: ....
Rating 1-10 (10=best): ....
Personal remarks: ....

Tiger Best Bitter

Brewery: Everards
Colour: Bronze
Flavour: Rich malt, tangy
Potency: 4.2% ABV

Date/place tasted: ....
Rating 1-10 (10=best): ....
Personal remarks: ....

Stones Best Bitter

Brewery: Bass
Colour: Straw
Flavour: Delicate, bitter finish
Potency: 4.1% ABV

Date/place tasted: ....
Rating 1-10 (10=best): ....
Personal remarks: ....

Brakspear SBA

Brewery: W H Brakspear & Sons
Colour: Coppery
Flavour: Rich malt & hop
Potency: 4% ABV

Date/place tasted: ....
Rating 1-10 (10=best): ....
Personal remarks: ....

Old Growler

Brewery: Nethergate
Colour: Dark
Flavour: Smooth, hints of chocolate
Potency: 5.8% ABV

Date/place tasted: ....
Rating 1-10 (10=best): ....
Personal remarks: ....

Badger Best Bitter

Brewery: Hall & Woodhouse Ltd
Colour: Copper
Flavour: Ripe, hoppy
Potency: 4% ABV

Date/place tasted: ....
Rating 1-10 (10=best): ....
Personal remarks: ....

Exmoor Gold

Brewery: Exmoor Ales Ltd
Colour: Golden
Flavour: Dry, bitter sweet
Potency: 4.5% ABV

Date/place tasted: ....
Rating 1-10 (10=best): ....
Personal remarks: ....

Tetley Dark Mild

Brewery: Tetley Walker
Colour: Dark
Flavour: Chewy malt
Potency: 2.9% ABV

Date/place tasted: ....
Rating 1-10 (10=best): ....
Personal remarks: ....

CARIBBEAN

Red Stripe

Brewery: Desnoes & Geddes (Jamaica)
Colour: Golden
Flavour: Light, fruity
Potency: 11.8 degrees

Date/place tasted: ....
Rating 1-10 (10=best): ....
Personal remarks: ....

Dragon Stout

Brewery: Desnoes & Geddes
Colour: Dark black
Flavour: Malty, strong
Potency: 17 degrees

Date/place tasted: ....
Rating 1-10 (10=best): ....
Personal remarks: ....

CANADA

True Bock

Brewery: Upper Canada Brewing Co.
Colour: Tawny
Flavour: Coffee, dry
Potency: 16 degrees

Date/place tasted: ....
Rating 1-10 (10=best): ....
Personal remarks: ....

CZECHOSLOVAKIA

Kapucin

Brewery: Vratislavice
Colour: Reddish/Black
Flavour: Bittersweet
Potency: 12 degrees

Date/place tasted: ....
Rating 1-10 (10=best): ....
Personal remarks: ....

Budweiser-Budvar

Brewery: Budejovice
Colour: Light Amber
Flavour: Sweet/Hoppy
Potency: 16 degrees

Date/place tasted: ....
Rating 1-10 (10=best): ....
Personal remarks: ....

DENMARK

Red Label

Brewery: Tuborg
Colour: Amber
Flavour: Malty
Potency: 10.7 degrees

Date/place tasted: ....
Rating 1-10 (10=best): ....
Personal remarks: ....

Imperial Stout

Brewery: Carlsberg
Colour: Dark
Flavour: Burnt toffee
Potency: 20 degrees

Date/place tasted: ....
Rating 1-10 (10=best): ....
Personal remarks: ....

Gammel Carlsberg Special Dark Lager

Brewery: Carlsberg
Colour: Dark Amber
Flavour: Tasty, malty
Potency: 10.7 degrees

Date/place tasted: ....
Rating 1-10 (10=best): ....
Personal remarks: ....

Gammel Jysk Porter

Brewery: Ceres
Colour: Dark
Flavour: Fruity
Potency: 20 degrees

Date/place tasted: ....
Rating 1-10 (10=best): ....
Personal remarks: ....

Paskebryg

Brewery: Tuborg
Colour: Pale gold
Flavour: Strong
Potency: 17.3 degrees

Date/place tasted: ....
Rating 1-10 (10=best): ....
Personal remarks: ....

Easter beer

Brewery: Carlsberg
Colour: Full
Flavour: Sweet and malty, dry
Potency: 18 degrees

Date/place tasted: ....
Rating 1-10 (10=best): ....
Personal remarks: ....

Let Pilsner

Brewery: Carlsberg
Colour: Pale
Flavour: Sweet, buttery
Potency: 7.7 degrees

Date/place tasted: ....
Rating 1-10 (10=best): ....
Personal remarks: ....

Green Beer

Brewery: Neptun
Colour: Green
Flavour: Soft, dry
Potency: 13 degrees

Date/place tasted: ....
Rating 1-10 (10=best): ....
Personal remarks: ....

Carlsberg Special Brew

Brewery: Carlsberg
Colour: Pale
Flavour: Strong
Potency: 19.2 degrees

Date/place tasted: ....
Rating 1-10 (10=best): ....
Personal remarks: ....

FINLAND

Koff Extra Strong Export

Brewery: Koff
Colour: Pale
Flavour: Aromatic
Potency: 15.5 degrees

Date/place tasted: ....
Rating 1-10 (10=best): ....
Personal remarks: ....

Christmas beer

Brewery: Koff
Colour: Amber red
Flavour: Clean, hoppy
Potency: 13.5 degrees

Date/place tasted: ....
Rating 1-10 (10=best): ....
Personal remarks: ....

Vaakuna

Brewery: Olvi
Colour: Full, golden
Flavour: Malty, toffee
Potency: 13.4 degrees

Date/place tasted: ....
Rating 1-10 (10=best): ....
Personal remarks: ....

FRANCE

La Biere du Demon

Brewery: Enfants de Gayant
Colour: Golden
Flavour: Dry, honey
Potency: 21.7 degrees

Date/place tasted: ....
Rating 1-10 (10=best): ....
Personal remarks: ....

Brune

Brewery: Pelforth
Colour: Deep claret
Flavour: Malty
Potency: 17.3 degrees

Date/place tasted: ....
Rating 1-10 (10=best): ....
Personal remarks: ....

Jubilator

Brewery: Schutzenberger's
Colour: Pale
Flavour: Fresh, fruity
Potency: 16 degrees

Date/place tasted: ....
Rating 1-10 (10=best): ....
Personal remarks: ....

GERMANY

Spaten Dunkel Export

Brewery: Spaten
Colour: Dark mahogany
Flavour: Medium full
Potency: 12.7 degrees

Date/place tasted: ....
Rating 1-10 (10=best): ....
Personal remarks: ....

Einbecker Hell

Brewery: Einbecker Brauhaus
Colour: Pale
Flavour: Smooth maltiness
Potency: 16.7 degrees

Date/place tasted: ....
Rating 1-10 (10=best): ....
Personal remarks: ....

Konig Ludvig Dunkel

Brewery: Kaltenberg
Colour: Dark
Flavour: Malty/Coffee-ish
Potency: 12 degrees

Date/place tasted: ....
Rating 1-10 (10=best): ....
Personal remarks: ....

Munchner Hell

Brewery: Spaten
Colour: Golden
Flavour: Malty
Potency: 12 degrees

Date/place tasted: ....
Rating 1-10 (10=best): ....
Personal remarks: ....

Spatengold

Brewery: Spaten
Colour: Amber/Gold
Flavour: Bitter
Potency: 13 degrees

Date/place tasted: ....
Rating 1-10 (10=best): ....
Personal remarks: ....

Marzenbier

Brewery: Spaten
Colour: Reddish
Flavour: Bitter
Potency: 13.5 degrees

Date/place tasted: ....
Rating 1-10 (10=best): ....
Personal remarks: ....

HUNGARY

Kobanyai

Brewery: Kobanyai
Colour: Light
Flavour: Hoppy
Potency: 11 degrees

Date/place tasted: ....
Rating 1-10 (10=best): ....
Personal remarks: ....

IRELAND

Guinness

Brewery: Guinness
Colour: Dark
Flavour: Roasty, hoppy
Potency: 1038 OG

Date/place tasted: ....
Rating 1-10 (10=best): ....
Personal remarks: ....

Murphy's Irish Stout

Brewery: Murphy - Lady's Well
Colour: Dark
Flavour: Lightly roasty
Potency: 1040 OG

Date/place tasted: ....
Rating 1-10 (10=best): ....
Personal remarks: ....

ITALY

La Rossa

Brewery: Moretti
Colour: Copper
Flavour: Rich, malty
Potency: 18 degrees

Date/place tasted: ....
Rating 1-10 (10=best): ....
Personal remarks: ....

La Bruna

Brewery: Moretti
Colour: Dark brown
Flavour: Tasty
Potency: 16 degrees

Date/place tasted: ....
Rating 1-10 (10=best): ....
Personal remarks: ....

JAPAN

Sapporo

Brewery: Sapporo
Colour: Pale
Flavour: Hoppy aroma
Potency: 4.5% ABV

Date/place tasted: ....
Rating 1-10 (10=best): ....
Personal remarks: ....

Kirin Lager Beer

Brewery: Kirin
Colour: Golden
Flavour: Hoppy
Potency: 1044 OG

Date/place tasted: ....
Rating 1-10 (10=best): ....
Personal remarks: ....

Kirin Stout

Brewery: Kirin
Colour: Dark
Flavour: Treacle toffee
Potency: 18 degrees

Date/place tasted: ....
Rating 1-10 (10=best): ....
Personal remarks: ....

MALTA

Hopleaf

Brewery: Farson
Colour: Pale
Flavour: Dry
Potency: 1040 OG

Date/place tasted: ....
Rating 1-10 (10=best): ....
Personal remarks: ....

NETHERLANDS

Heineken

Brewery: Heineken
Colour: Pale golden
Flavour: Light, fruity
Potency: 5% ABV

Date/place tasted: ....
Rating 1-10 (10=best): ....
Personal remarks: ....

Grolsch

Brewery: Grolsche
Colour: Pale gold
Flavour: Fresh hay
Potency: 5% ABV

Date/place tasted: ....
Rating 1-10 (10=best): ....
Personal remarks: ....

Capucijn

Brewery: Budels
Colour: Pale
Flavour: Applewood
Potency: 16 degrees

Date/place tasted: ....
Rating 1-10 (10=best): ....
Personal remarks: ....

Imperator

Brewery: Brand
Colour: Amber
Flavour: Malty
Potency: 17.5 degrees

Date/place tasted: ....
Rating 1-10 (10=best): ....
Personal remarks: ....

Double Bock

Brewery: Brand
Colour: Beaujolais
Flavour: Rich
Potency: 18.5 degrees

Date/place tasted: ....
Rating 1-10 (10=best): ....
Personal remarks: ....

NEW ZEALAND

Steinlager

Brewery: New Zealand Breweries
Colour: Golden
Flavour: Mildly dry
Potency: 11.3 degrees

Date/place tasted: ....
Rating 1-10 (10=best): ....
Personal remarks: ....

Rheineck

Brewery: New Zealand Breweries
Colour: Golden
Flavour: Sweetish
Potency: 9.8 degrees

Date/place tasted: ....
Rating 1-10 (10=best): ....
Personal remarks: ....

Lion Red

Brewery: Lion
Colour: Full
Flavour: Malty note
Potency: 9 degrees

Date/place tasted: ....
Rating 1-10 (10=best): ....
Personal remarks: ....

SPAIN

San Miguel

Brewery: San Miguel
Colour: Light
Flavour: Smooth
Potency: 12 degrees

Date/place tasted: ....
Rating 1-10 (10=best): ....
Personal remarks: ....

SWEDEN

Carnegie Porter

Brewery: Prypps
Colour: Coffee
Flavour: Rich, roasty
Potency: 10.2 degrees

Date/place tasted: ....
Rating 1-10 (10=best): ....
Personal remarks: ....

SWITZERLAND

Samiclaus

Brewery: Hurlimann
Colour: Reddish
Flavour: Malty, full
Potency: 27.6 degrees !!!

Date/place tasted: ....
Rating 1-10 (10=best): ....
Personal remarks: ....

Hexenbrau

Brewery: Hurlimann
Colour: Dark
Flavour: Malty, burnt toffee
Potency: 13.5 degrees

Date/place tasted: ....
Rating 1-10 (10=best): ....
Personal remarks: ....

Albani Brau

Brewery: Haldengut
Colour: Dark red
Flavour: Lightly fruity
Potency: 19.0 degrees

Date/place tasted: ....
Rating 1-10 (10=best): ....
Personal remarks: ....

USA

Budweiser

Brewery: Anheuser-Busch
Colour: Light gold
Flavour: Mildly sweet
Potency: 4.0% ABV

Date/place tasted: ....
Rating 1-10 (10=best): ....
Personal remarks: ....

Miller Pilsner

Brewery: Miller
Colour: Light gold
Flavour: Clean, faintly fruity
Potency: 4.2% ABV

Date/place tasted: ....
Rating 1-10 (10=best): ....
Personal remarks: ....

Michelob

Brewery: Anheuser-Busch
Colour: Light amber
Flavour: Slightly hoppy, light
Potency: 4.9% ABV

Date/place tasted: ....
Rating 1-10 (10=best): ....
Personal remarks: ....

Signature

Brewery: Stroh
Colour: Pale gold
Flavour: Dry, slightly fruity
Potency: 4.8% ABV

Date/place tasted: ....
Rating 1-10 (10=best): ....
Personal remarks: ....

Steam Beer

Brewery: Anchor
Colour: Golden
Flavour: Fruity
Potency: 4.0% ABV

Date/place tasted: ....
Rating 1-10 (10=best): ....
Personal remarks: ....

Old Foghorn

Brewery: Anchor
Colour: Amber
Flavour: Malty, fruity
Potency: 7.0% ABV

Date/place tasted: ....
Rating 1-10 (10=best): ....
Personal remarks: ....

GLOSSARY OF BEER TERMS

To some, beer is beer is beer. But to others, each brew can be identified as belonging to a particular category of beers. If you've ever wondered what the difference is between a Bock and a Kriek, here is a glossary of some of the terms regularly used by beer buffs around the world...

Abbey beer, a strong fruity ale brewed in Belgium, inspired by the handiwork of the Trappist Monks.

Additives, used to clarify or preserve beers. Not fashionable.

Ale, the relatively quick, warm fermentation produces a fruity accent, utilising a strain of yeast which rises during the procedure. This is known as top fermentation and thus defines the product as an ale. There are many types, varying in strength and colour.

- **Brown Ale,** there are two variants in Britain based on levels of sweetness. A Belgian variety exists, having a sweet-sour taste.

- **Cream Ale,** golden, sweetish and very mild, produced in the U.S.A. An ideal socialising drink.

- **India Pale Ale,** super premium, fruity, hoppy pale ale.

- **Light Ale,** this is an alternative term for bottled bitter in England, whereas in Scotland it refers to a dark ale.

- **Scotch Ale,** very malty. Best known for its strength.

- **Old Ale,** a British name for a medium strength dark ale. Note, however, that any dark ale in Australia is known as 'old'.

- **Pale Ale,** this English ale is fruity and copper coloured.

Alt, a German word meaning old.

Barley, used for brewing ale since 4000 BC.

Barley Wine, very strong English ale.

Beer, lagers, ales, stouts and similar are all beers, since they are all brewed using malted grain and seasoned with hops.

Biere de Garde, variety brewed in the north west of France. A member of the ale family, it is fruity. Medium strength.

Bitter, dry ale usually served on draught in a straight pint glass, ideal temperature 12-13°C (54-55F).

Bock, a potent lager ideal in late autumn & winter. Should be served at less 9°C and be drunk from a stoneware mug.

Diat Pils, the thorough fermentation process absorbs carbohydrates and creates alcohol, therefore ideal for diabetics but not slimmers. The process produces a very dry, strongish beer, with the pilsner type being the best example.

Dortmunder, can be any beer brewed in Dortmund, but the city is especially known for the Export style.

Export, means 'premium'. The exception to this is in Germany where it is a pale, dry lager.

Framboise, this is a raspberry Lambic. Served in champagne flutes, lightly chilled.

Hefe, describes a sedimented beer. German prefix for yeast.

Helles, German for pale.

Hops, are added to the fermentation process to produce true 'Beer' as opposed to Ale.

Imperial "Russian Stout", rich stout which has a fruity, 'burnt' flavour.

Kriek, a dry almondy, cherry Lambic.

Lager, often applied to 'basic' beers, but generally any bottom-fermented beers.

Lambic, brewed in Belgium it is a spontaneously-fermenting beer.

Light Beer, this is an American watery, low-cal version of the Pilsner style beer.

Malt Liquor, a strong American lager which is most often brewed cheaply, and with high sugar levels. It is neither, as the name suggests, a liquor nor is it malty. It is usually consumed to get drunk quickly.

Mead, fermented from honey and water.

Mild, a lightly hopped English ale. Dark and normally of low strength.

Pilsener, a fragrant, dry pale lager inspired by the original Pilsener from Czechoslovakia. Any dry, pale lager of medium gravity is often given this name.

Porter, brewed in London this is top-fermenting and almost black in colour.

Saison, slightly sour, medium strength, summer ale brewed in Belgium.

Steam Beer, produced by the Anchor Brewery in San Francisco, has a unique blend of lager and ale.

Stout, a black roasty top-fermented restorative brewed in England, usually sweet. In Ireland it is usually much drier.

Trappist, the Belgian and Dutch Trappist Monks brew sedimented strong and fruity ales which possess a port-like quality.

Urquell, German for 'the original source of'.

Weissbier, a German term used for wheat or 'white' beers.

White Beer, a common name for wheat beers.

Yeast, tiny fungus organisms used to turn sugar into alcohol.

Answers to the Beer Lover's Quiz on page 53.

1. Belgium.
2. Laidly Gold wheat beer.
3. With Bede-ales.
4. Jedediah Buxton.
5. To obtain cash or wedding presents.
6. Iceland.
7. Kaiser Wilhelm of Germany.
8. 5.5°C
9. Strychnine.
10. Mesopotamia.
11. Western Australia.
12. 16.9%
13. Cock Ale.
14. The Sumerians.
15. Kirin.

Royal Proclamation

In 1436 a Royal writ ordered the Sheriffs of London to proclaim that *"the drink called beere is a notable, healthy and temperate drink"* - and anyone who said otherwise faced severe punishment.

MORE HUMOUR TITLES...

The Hangover Handbook & Boozer's Bible
(Also in the shape of a beercan)
Ever groaned, burped and cursed the morning after, as Vesuvius erupted in your stomach, a bass drummer thumped on your brain and a canary fouled its nest in your throat? Then you need these 100+ hangover remedies. There's an exclusive Hangover Ratings Chart, a Boozer's Calendar, a Hangover Clinic, and you can meet the Great Drunks of History, try the Boozer's Reading Chart, etc., etc. £3.99

The Drinker's IQ Test
Have you ever wondered if drink is affecting your brain? Then this book will confirm your worst fears or give you a clean bill of health. Do you know how much pub crisps work out at per tonne? What would you do if a German gave you two-fingers? How much beer can anybody drink on an empty stomach? And while you are thinking, there's a collection of the world's best drinking jokes to relax your brain. £3.99

If you would rather not damage your copy of The Beerlover's Bible, please use plain paper and remember to include all the details listed below!

Please send me a copy of

I enclose a cheque/payment made payable to 'Take That Ltd'. **Postage is free within the U.K.** Please add £1 per title in other EEC countries and £3 elsewhere.

Name:_____

Address:_____

_____

_____

Postcode:_____

Please return to: **Take That Books, P.O.Box 200, Harrogate, HG1 4XB**

MORE HUMOUR TITLES...

The Ancient Art of Farting by Dr. C.Huff

Ever since time began, man (not woman) has farted. Does this ability lie behind many of the so far unexplained mysteries of history ? You Bet - because Dr. C.Huff's research shows conclusively there's something rotten about history taught in schools. If you do most of your reading on the throne, then this book is your ideal companion. Sit back and fart yourself silly as you split your sides laughing! £3.99

A Wunch of Bankers

Do you HATE BANKS? Then you need this collection of stories aimed directly at the crotch of your bank manager. A Wunch of Bankers mixes cartoons and jokes about banks with real-life horror stories of the bare-faced money-grabbing tactics of banks. If you think you've been treated badly, read these stories!!!! £3.99

How to Get Rid of Your Boss

No matter how much you love your work, there is always one person who makes your professional life a misery - your boss. But all that can change. Find out, with the use of helpful diagrams and cartoons, how to get rid of this person that you despise. It's your chance to get your own back and really break free! £3.99

The Bog Book

(in the shape of a toilet seat)

How much time do you spend in the bog every day? Are you letting valuable time go to waste? Not any longer! Now you can spend every second to your advantage. The Bog Book is packed with enough of the funny, the weird and the wonderful to drive you POTTY. Fill your brain while you empty your bowels... £3.99